*A thought may touch the edge of our life with light.*

—JOHN TROWBRIDGE (1827-1916)
*American writer*

To My Dear Friend,

You are a very special support and
friend to me Cheryl.
I hope you inspiration and growth
in using this journal as journaling
is very often the path to very deep
understanding.

Love
Lorraine

December 1991.

# PASSAGES
# JOURNAL

*All glory comes from daring to begin.*
—ANONYMOUS

*Life is not complex. We are complex. Life is simple, and the simple thing is the right thing.*

—OSCAR WILDE (1854-1900)
*Irish writer*

*If you have made mistakes . . . there is always another chance for you . . . You may have a fresh start any moment you choose, for this thing we call "failure" is not the falling down, but the staying down.*

—MARY PICKFORD (1893-1979)
*American actress*

*The world is a rose; smell it and pass it to your friends.*
—PERSIAN PROVERB

*Keep constantly in mind in how many things you yourself have already witnessed changes. The universe is change, life is understanding.*

—MARCUS AURELIUS (121-180 A.D.)
*Roman emperor and philosopher*

*Not until we are lost do we begin to understand ourselves.*

—HENRY DAVID THOREAU (1817-1862)
*American naturalist and writer*

Birds sing after a storm; why shouldn't people feel as free to delight in whatever remains to them?

—ROSE FITZGERALD KENNEDY, b. 1890
*Mother of President John F. Kennedy*

*In the midst of winter, I finally learned that there was in me an invincible summer.*

—ALBERT CAMUS (1913-1960)
*French writer and existentialist*

*We are all pilgrims on the same journey . . . but some pilgrims have better road maps.*

—NELSON DE MILLE, b. 1943
*American writer*

*It doesn't matter if the water is cold or warm if you're going to have to wade through it anyway.*

—TEILHARD DE CHARDIN (1881-1955)
*French paleontologist and philosopher*

*From without, no wonderful effect is wrought within ourselves unless some interior, responding wonder meets it.*

—HERMAN MELVILLE (1819-1891)
*American writer*

*There are two things to aim at in life: first, to get what you want; and after that, to enjoy it. Only the wisest of mankind achieve the second.*

—LOGAN PEARSALL SMITH (1865-1946)
*American writer*

*It had been my repeated experience that when you said to life calmly and firmly (but very firmly!), "I trust you; do what you must," life had an uncanny way of responding to your need.*

—OLGA ILYIN
*Russian-American writer*

*Life is too short to be little.*
—BENJAMIN DISRAELI (1804-1881)
*English statesman and writer*

*That is what learning is. You suddenly understand some-*
*thing you've understood all your life, but in a new way.*

—DORIS LESSING, b. 1919
*English writer*

*Real development is not leaving things behind, as on a road, but drawing life from them, as from a root.*

—G.K. CHESTERTON (1874-1936)
*English writer*

*I learn by going where I have to go.*

—THEODORE ROETHKE (1908-1963)
*American poet*

*The events of childhood do not pass, but repeat themselves like seasons of the year.*

—ELEANOR FARJEON (1881-1965)
*English writer*

*You were once wild here. Don't let them tame you!*

—ISADORA DUNCAN (1878-1927)
*American dancer*

*Each day, and the living of it, has to be a conscious creation in which discipline and order are relieved with some play and pure foolishness.*

—MAY SARTON (1912-1985)
*Belgian-American writer*

The years teach much which the days never know.

—RALPH WALDO EMERSON (1803-1882)
*American writer and philospher*

*Accept the pain, cherish the joys, resolve the regrets; then can come the best of benedictions—"If I had my life to live over, I'd do it all the same."*

—JOAN McINTOSH, b. 1943
*American writer*

*Life seems to be a never-ending series of survivals, doesn't it?*

—CARROLL BAKER, b. 1931
*American actress and writer*

*And remember, we all stumble, every one of us. That's why it's a comfort to go hand in hand.*

—E. K. BROUGH
*American writer*

*If I were to begin life again, I should want it as it were.*
*I would only open my eyes a little more.*

—JULES RENARD (1864-1910)
*French writer*

*Growth, in some curious way, I suspect, depends on being always in motion just a little bit, one way or another.*

—NORMAN MAILER, b. 1923
*American writer*

Some trees grow very tall and straight and large in the forest close to each other, but some must stand by themselves or they won't grow at all.

—OLIVER WENDELL HOLMES (1809-1894)
*American writer*

*What would life be if we had no courage to attempt anything?*

—VINCENT VAN GOGH (1853-1890)
*Dutch painter*

Experience is not what happens to you; it is what you do with what happens to you.

—ALDOUS HUXLEY (1894-1963)
*English writer*

*If we are always arriving and departing, it is also true that we are eternally anchored. One's destination is never a place, but rather a new way of looking at things.*

—HENRY MILLER (1891-1980)
*American writer*

*If I shoot at the sun, I may hit a star.*

—P. T. BARNUM (1810-1891)
*American showman*

*Do not think your truth can be found by anyone else.*
—ANDRÉ GIDE (1869-1951)
*French writer*

*I began to have an idea of my life, not as the slow shaping of achievement to fit my preconceived purposes, but as the gradual discovery and growth of a purpose which I did not know.*

—JOANNA FIELD, b. 1900
*English psychologist*

*Very little is needed to make a happy life. It is all within yourself, in your way of thinking.*

—MARCUS AURELIUS (121-180 A.D.)
*Roman emperor and philosopher*

*Be not afraid of growing slowly, be afraid only of standing still.*

—CHINESE PROVERB

*We must have the courage to allow a little disorder in our lives.*

—BEN WEININGER, M.D. and
HENRY RABIN, D.D.
*Contemporary American writers*

*Perspective, I soon realized, was a fine commodity, but utterly useless when I was in the thick of things.*
—INGRID BENGIS, b. 1944
*American writer*

*And the trouble is, if you don't risk anything
you risk even more.*

—ERICA JONG, b. 1942
*American writer and feminist*

*If only I may grow: firmer, simpler—quieter, warmer.*

—DAG HAMMARSKJÖLD (1905-1961)
*Swedish statesman and humanitarian*

*It is not how much we have, but how much we enjoy,
that makes happiness.*

—CHARLES H. SPURGEON (1834-1892)
*English clergyman*

*No one remains quite what he was when he recognizes himself.*

—THOMAS MANN (1875-1955)
*German writer*

*When it is dark enough, you can see the stars.*

—RALPH WALDO EMERSON (1803-1882)
*American writer and philosopher*

*I was raised to sense what someone wanted me to be and be that kind of person. It took me a long time not to judge myself through someone else's eyes.*

—SALLY FIELD, b. 1946
*American actress*

*A life spent in making mistakes is not only more honorable but more useful than a life spent in doing nothing.*

—GEORGE BERNARD SHAW (1856-1950)
*Irish dramatist and critic*

*He who masters the grey everyday is a hero.*
—FYODOR DOSTOYEVSKY (1821-1881)
*Russian writer*

*There are two rules in life . . . One, things never work out all the way. And two, they always turn around.*

—JAMES WEBB, (1946-1980)
*Scottish writer*

*My body has an age, but I don't.*

—BEN WEININGER, M.D. and
HENRY RABIN, D.D.
*Contemporary American writers*

*I am incapable of conceiving infinity, and yet I do not accept finity. I want this adventure that is the context of my life to go on without end.*

—SIMONE DE BEAUVOIR (1908-1986)
*French writer*

*You must do the thing you think you cannot do.*
—ELEANOR ROOSEVELT (1884-1962)
*American stateswoman and humanitarian*

It's not when you realize that nothing can help you—
religion, pride, anything—it's when you realize you don't
need any aid.

—WILLIAM FAULKNER (1897-1962)
*American writer*

*I think it's the end of progress if you stand still and think of what you've done in the past. I keep on.*

—LESLIE CARON (1931–1988)
*French actress*

*All things are possible until they are proved impossible—
and even the impossible may only be so, as of now.*

—PEARL S. BUCK (1892-1973)
*American writer and humanitarian*

*The only courage that matters is the kind that gets you from one minute to the next.*

—MIGNON McLAUGHLIN
*American writer*

*Everything in life that we really accept undergoes a change.*

—KATHERINE MANSFIELD (1888-1923)
*English writer*

*Life can only be understood backwards,
but it must be lived forwards.*

—SØREN AABYE KIERKEGAARD (1813-1855)
*Danish philosopher*

*If we could be twice young and twice old, we could correct all our mistakes.*

—EURIPIDES (c.484-406 B.C.)
*Greek dramatist*

*If fate throws a knife at you, there are two ways of catching it—by the blade and by the handle.*

—ORIENTAL PROVERB

*The day will happen whether or not you get up.*
—JOHN CIARDI (1916-1985)
*American poet and critic*

*Mingle a little folly with your wisdom; a little nonsense now and then is pleasant.*

—HORACE (65-8 B.C.)
*Roman poet and satirist*

*. . . When you're not thinking about yourself a lot, you're usually happy.*

—AL PACINO, b. 1940
*American actor*

*That which we are, we are, and if we are ever to be any better, now is the time to begin.*

—ALFRED, LORD TENNYSON (1809-1892)
*English poet*

*Habit is habit, and not to be flung out the window by man, but coaxed downstairs a step at a time.*

—MARK TWAIN (1835-1910)
*American humorist and writer*

*It isn't so much that hard times are coming; the change observed is mostly soft times going.*

—GROUCHO MARX (1890-1977)
*American humorist, actor, and writer*

*Trying to define yourself is like trying to bite your own teeth.*

—ALAN WATTS, b. 1915
*American philosopher*

We grow neither better nor worse as we get old,
but more like ourselves.

—MAY LAMBERTON BECKER (1873-1958)
*American writer and critic*

*The best we can do for one another is to exchange our thoughts freely; and that, after all, is about all.*

—JAMES A. FROUDE (1818-1894)
*English historian*

*The important thing is not to stop questioning.*

—ALBERT EINSTEIN (1879-1955)
*German-born American physicist*

We are made out of oppositions; we live between two poles . . . you don't reconcile the poles, you just recognize them.

—ORSON WELLES (1915-1985)
*American film director*

... *Words are a form of action, capable of influencing change. Their articulation represents a complete, lived experience.*

—INGRID BENGIS, b. 1944
American writer

*Be happy. It's one way of being wise.*
—COLETTE (1873-1954)
*French writer*

*To know how to grow old is the master work of wisdom, and one of the most difficult chapters in the great art of living.*

—HENRI FRÉDÉRIC AMIEL (1821-1881)
*Swiss poet and philosopher*

*Our greatest glory consists, not in never falling, but in rising every time we fall.*

—OLIVER GOLDSMITH (1728-1774)
*English poet and writer*

*For every problem there is one solution which is simple, neat, and wrong.*

—H. L. MENCKEN (1880-1956)
*American editor and satirist*

*The best way out is always through.*

—ROBERT FROST (1874-1963)
*American poet*

*You can't change the music of your soul.*
—KATHARINE HEPBURN, b. 1909
*American actress*

*I've dreamt in my life dreams that have stayed with me ever after, and changed my ideas; they've gone through and through me, like wine through water, and altered the colour of my mind.*

—EMILY BRONTË (1818-1848)
*English writer*

*Of all the liars in the world, sometimes the worst are your own fears.*

—RUDYARD KIPLING (1865-1936)
*English poet and writer*

When you're an orthodox worrier, some days
are worse than others.

—ERMA BOMBECK, b. 1927
*American humorist*

*When you have to make a choice and don't make it, that is in itself a choice.*

—WILLIAM JAMES (1842-1910)
*American psychologist and philosopher*

*Nothing is as far away as one minute ago.*

—JIM BISHOP (1907-1987)
*American writer*

To feel *that* one *has* a place *in* life *solves half the problem* of contentment.

—GEORGE E. WOODBERR (1855-1930)
*American writer*

*Anything you're good at contributes to happiness.*

—BERTRAND RUSSELL (1872-1970)
*English mathematician and philosopher*

*We grow in time to trust the future for our answers.*

—RUTH BENEDICT (1887-1948)
*American anthropologist*

*Any life, no matter how long and complex it may be, is made up of a single moment—the moment in which a man finds out, once and for all, who he is.*

—JORGE LUIS BORGES (1899-1986)
*Argentine writer*

*The difficulty in life is the choice.*

—GEORGE MOORE (1852-1933)
*Irish writer*

*Risk is what separates the good part of life from the tedium.*

—JIMMY ZERO
*American musician*

*What you get is a living—what you give is a life.*

—LILLIAN GISH, b. 1896
*American actress*

*Life begets life. Energy creates energy. It is by spending oneself that one becomes rich.*

—SARAH BERNHARDT (1844-1923)
*French actress*

*People change and forget to tell each other.*
—LILLIAN HELLMAN (1907-1984)
*American dramatist and writer*

*The hardest of all is learning to be a well of affection,
and not a fountain, to show them that we love them, not
when we feel like it, but when they do.*

—NAN FAIRBROTHER, (1913-1971)
*English writer and landscape architect*

*Life is a child playing around your feet, a tool you hold firmly in your grasp, a bench you sit down upon in the evening, in your garden.*

—JEAN ANOUILH (1910-1987)
*French dramatist and screenwriter*

*. . . Be glad you had the moment.*
—STEVE SHAGAN, b. 1927
*American screenwriter and film producer*

*Self-conquest is the greatest of all victories.*

—PLATO (c. 427-347 B.C.)
*Greek philosopher*